Grow Your Business:

Successful secrets to expand your Business Growth

By

Donald K. Morgan

Copyright © 2022 by Donald K. Morgan

All Rights Reserved.
No part of this book may be used or reproduced by any means, graphic, electronic, or mechanical, including photocopying, recording, taping, or by any information storage retrieval system without the written permission of the publisher.

Table of Content

INTRODUCTION

Chapter 1
What is the term "BUSINESS"

Chapter 2
How to Grow a Business

Chapter 3
Know your Customer

Chapter 4
The role of TRUST in

Business

Chapter 5
Follow Up your Customers

INTRODUCTION.

Any size of business searches for methods to improve sales and market share. To improve their business, companies frequently decide to employ various growth methods. Leading strategic initiatives for business success can be facilitated by your understanding of these tactics. This book explains the many company growth tactics now employed by businesses and offers suggestions to assist you in expanding your business.

Chapter 1

What is the term "BUSINESS"

The term "BUSINESS " refers to an organization or enterprising entity engaging in commercial, industrial, or professional activity. A business's goal is to coordinate some form of economic production (of goods or services). Businesses can be for-profit corporations or nonprofit organizations working to advance a social cause. Businesses are different in size and scope from small, local enterprises to enormous, global conglomerates.

A person's efforts and operations to produce and sell goods and services for profit are also referred to as business.

The term business much of the time implies a component that works for business, current, or master reasons. The thought begins with an idea and a name, and wide factual reviewing may be supposed to conclude that changing the idea into a business is so possible.

Associations as often as possible require field-tried techniques before exercises start. A field-tried methodology is a legitimate report that approaches the association's targets and targets and records the systems and plans to achieve these targets and objectives. Attractive systems are central when you really want to get the means to begin exercises.

Concluding the legal plan of the business is a

critical variable to consider, since business people could need to secure awards and licenses and follow selection necessities to begin genuine errands.

Endeavors are seen as juridical individuals in various countries, suggesting that the business can have property, accept commitment, and be sued in court.

Most associations work to make an advantage, routinely called for-benefit. Regardless, a couple of associations that have a target to drive a particular explanation without benefit are insinuated as not-for-advantage or good cause. These components could fill in as respectable objective, articulations, culture, enlightening, and donning adventures, political and support get-togethers, or social organizations affiliations.

Business practices much of the time integrate the arrangement and obtaining of work and items. Business activity can happen wherever, whether that is in a genuine retail exterior, on the web, or on a roadside. Anyone who conducts business activity with financial benefit ought to report this compensation to the Internal Revenue Service (IRS).

An association often portrays its business by the business where it works. For example, the land business, publicizing business, or dozing cushion creation business are occurrences of adventures. Business is a term often used to show trades concerning a major thing or organization. For example, ExxonMobil conducts its business by giving oil.

There are numerous ways of sorting out a business, and there are different lawful and tax collection structures that relate with these. Among others, organizations are ordinarily characterized and for the most part organized as:

Sole ownerships: As the name recommends, a sole ownership is possessed and worked by a solitary individual. There is no legitimate partition between the business and the proprietor, and that implies the assessment and lawful liabilities of the business are the obligation of the proprietor.

Partnership: A Partnership is a business connection between at least two individuals who together direct business. Each accomplice contributes assets and cash to the business and offers in the benefits and misfortunes of the business. The common benefits and misfortunes are recorded on each accomplice's expense form.

Corporation: A Corporation a business where a gathering goes about as a solitary substance. Proprietors are generally alluded to as investors who trade thought for the company's normal stock. Consolidating a business discharges proprietors of the monetary responsibility of business commitments. A partnership accompanies troublesome tax collection rules for the proprietors of the business.

Business Sizes
Autonomous organizations
Little owner worked associations are called

autonomous organizations. Generally directed by one individual or a little assembling with under 100 specialists,

These associations integrate family diners, privately settled associations, attire, books, and disseminating associations, and little creators. Beginning around 2021, 32.5

million confidential endeavors with 61.2 million agents were working in the United States.

The Small Business Administration (SBA) uses the amount of delegates working at an association and its yearly pay to formally portray a privately owned business. For 229 industry regions, from planning and gathering to food organization and land, the SBA sets assessing rules predictably.

Associations that satisfy the rules of the SBA can possess all the necessary qualities for advances, grants, and "privately owned business set-asides," contracts where the public government limits competition to help autonomous endeavors look for and win authoritative arrangements.

Moderate measured Enterprises
There is no legitimate assurance in the U.S. to describe a moderate measured or medium-sized association. In any case, when tremendous U.S. metropolitan networks like Philadelphia, Baltimore, and Boston survey the

location of working associations, a medium-sized association is described as one with 100 to 499 delegates or $10 million to under $50 million in yearly gross arrangements.

Enormous Businesses
Enormous associations consistently have more than 1000 delegates and acquire $50 something like million in gross receipts.

They could give corporate stock to back errands as a public partnership.

Enormous endeavors may be arranged in one country with overall errands. They are habitually organized by workplaces, similar to HR, finance, displaying, bargains, and imaginative work. Not in any way shape or form like pretty much nothing and medium measured adventures, guaranteed by an individual or get-together, immense affiliations often separate their tax collection rate from their owners, who commonly don't manage their associations yet in light of everything, a picked directorate lays out most business decisions.

How Do You Start a Business?

There are a few stages you really want to obstacle to begin a business. This incorporates leading statistical surveying, fostering a marketable strategy, looking for capital or different types of subsidizing, picking an area and business structure, picking the right name, submitting enlistment desk work, getting charge records (boss and citizen IDs), and pulling grants and licenses. It's likewise really smart to set up a ledger with a monetary establishment to work with your regular financial necessities.

How Do You Launch an Online Business? Beginning a web-based business includes a portion of similar strides as a customary business, with a couple of special cases.

You actually need to do your statistical surveying and foster a field-tested strategy prior to whatever else. Whenever that is finished, pick a name and construction for your business, then, at that point, record any desk work to enroll your association.

Instead of tracking down an actual area, pick a stage and plan your site. Prior to sending off your business, you ought to figure out how to develop your objective market, whether that is through customary showcasing means or more inventive ways like virtual entertainment.

How Do You Come Up With a Business Name? Your business name ought to fit the sort of association you intend to run and it ought to be snappy — something that individuals will incline toward and recall, also partner with you as well as the items and administrations you intend to sell. Inventiveness is vital. Furthermore, in particular, it ought to be a name that isn't now being used by another person. Go on the web and do a business name search to check whether it's accessible or currently enlisted.

How Do You Write a Business Plan?
Field-tested strategies are vital for maintaining your business and can assist you with getting the financing you really want to begin your tasks.

You can pick between a conventional or a lean marketable strategy.

A customary field-tested strategy is extremely extensive with a ton of subtleties. This incorporates a rundown of the organization and the manners in which it will succeed. It additionally incorporates data about your market, the board, items and administrations, promoting, and deals projections.

Lean arrangements are more limited yet at the same time contain extremely helpful data, for example, organization subtleties, layouts of the business exercises and client connections, cost designs, and income transfers.

You can find formats on the web or think of your marketable strategy record.

How Do You Get a Business Loan? Essential financing for a business frequently comes by means of a credit. A conventional bank or an administration upheld credit, for example, those presented through the Small

Business Administration are two choices. Imminent moneylenders need to see business subtleties, particularly for new companies. Ensure you have your marketable strategy prepared, including blueprints of expenses and income streams, and guarantee you have a decent FICO rating. You might have to put down a guarantee to get the credit on the off chance that you're supported.

The Bottom Line
Organizations are the foundation of an economy. They give items and administrations that can be bought by people and different organizations.

Organizations range in size from little to huge and work in various ventures. Business structures additionally shift from sole organizations to large companies that give investor value to their proprietors.

While beginning a business, properly investigate things and foster a marketable strategy. This permits you to collect the cash you want to begin your activity.

Chapter 2

How to Grow a Business

Business of any size search for ways of extending their piece of the pie and increment incomes. Organizations frequently decide to carry out unambiguous development techniques to propel their business. Understanding these systems can assist you with driving key drives for organization development. In this article we make sense of the sorts of business development procedures utilized by organizations today with thoughts to assist you with developing your association.

What is business Growth? Business growth is a peculiarity that happens when entrepreneurs, representatives and outside factors impact the outcome of an organization. A business develops when it extends a client base, builds income or delivers more item.

Growth is the objective of most organizations and is the explanation for some choices that influence the day to day operations of an organization both inside and remotely. Business development is influenced by buyer patterns, market valuable open doors and choices made by organization administration.

Growing a business takes arranging and thought endeavors that fall into these fundamental classifications:

- Natural: Organic development happens when a business makes the right circumstances for extension. This incorporates genuinely extending office space to consider organization development or expanding item contributions.

- Vital: An essential

methodology centers around long haul development through unambiguous drives. Organizations frequently move into this development stage after a time of natural development. Organizations might attempt to acquire an offer in undiscovered business sectors or plan to deliver new stock.

- Organization/consolidation: This sort of procedure happens when an organization gets together with one more business to set out more market open doors.
Inside: An inner development technique is one that attempts to

amplify inward cycles to build business and income.

14 sorts of business Growth techniques

Here are the primary strategies organizations can use to extend their portion of the overall industry, incomes and inside processes:

- Market infiltration
Market infiltration

happens when a business attempts to create further development inside their ongoing business sector. To do this they might attempt to bring down costs or increment promoting endeavors to acquire portion of the overall industry. Expanding brand mindfulness can be a successful method for carrying out this system.

- Item advancement

Organizations might pick a development procedure that includes improving current items or making new ones to increment income. A few organizations decide to take existing stock and add new elements to draw in additional clients. Putting resources into the plan and formation of new items is one way organizations encourage development.

• Market development In the market extension strategy, a business attempts to extend in their ongoing business sector by arriving at undiscovered client bases. For instance, an office supply organization might attempt to acquire piece of the pie by offering to instructive foundations, medical care associations and government offices rather than stringently offering to corporate office clients.

- Vertical coordination Organizations who choose to development through vertical coordination techniques take on one more piece of the assembling or dispersion process. This might imply that an organization starts to create their own bundling materials or purchases a plant that delivers a critical thing for an item.

- Efficiency and proficiency

A few organizations develop by changing their cycles to increment efficiency. Effective creation techniques can assist with reducing expenses and increment income. A business might decide to direct a review of their assembling processes, conveyance techniques and different pieces of their creation chain.

- New geologies Putting promoting endeavors into development in different areas can likewise be a development system for organizations. This can mean territorial, public or even overall development of item contributions and conveyance. Offering items beyond an ongoing topographical region can produce new income streams on the off chance that circulation is likewise taken care of successfully.

- Portion of wallet

By zeroing in on client maintenance and quality assistance, organizations can start development by extending deals to current clients. Offering to existing clients commonly costs not exactly other advertising endeavors. This procedure can be compelling for organizations with fantastic client care rehearses and a faithful client base.

• Enhancement Organizations that decide to develop through enhancement make new items for a totally new market. This sort of development might mean moving into global business sectors or regions where the organization has no earlier deals history. A few organizations do this by searching for areas of enormous scope extension, expecting to acquire portion of the overall industry. Enhanced organizations might possess a stake in various ventures through a scope of item contributions.

- Acquisitions Organizations might execute a development

system by purchasing another business. An organization could purchase out a contender to retain their piece of the pie and obtain their resources. The parent organization will then encounter development in deals and income. This technique energizes more quick development on the grounds that a business is basically getting involved with a market as opposed to focusing on natural development strategies.

• New channels Offering items through new dissemination channels is one more way for organizations to grow. For instance, an organization might choose to offer item in retail locations subsequent to working solely on the web. An organization may likewise choose to work with purchasers as opposed to offering only business to business.

• New plans of action Impacting the manner in which you carry on with work can influence development designs in an organization. At the point when a business chooses to roll out functional improvements, they get the opportunity to set out more development open doors utilizing different procedures.

• Speculation Claiming offers and putting resources into different organizations might be a method for extending business development. At the point
when an organization utilizes their income to expand the resources of

another business, they have the valuable chance to get benefits as a partner. This might incorporate profits, investment opportunities or other venture income.

• Market division
By zeroing in on a little fragment of industry and filling explicitly around there, organizations frequently track down potential

learning experiences. Private ventures can profit from this procedure in business sectors where huge organizations as of now overwhelm an enormous piece of the piece of the pie.

- Business organizations

Vital associations can increment business development by utilizing the critical components of at least two brands. In this methodology, organizations frequently make an agreement with clear terms illustrating the understanding for the two players. Organizations from various enterprises or markets benefit from acquiring the consideration of another customer bunch.

Ways to help your business grow
Here are a few plans to assist with growing your business:

- Understand your Audience: One method for empowering development is to get to realize your client base. Track down key segment data by dissecting information from different sources. Search for ways of following your client's purchasing inclinations or administration contracts. When you comprehend this information, you can drive choices that influence income, for example, item contributions, portion of the overall industry and local extension.

- Center around driving Leads: Lead generation is a critical method for growing a business. Getting leads both naturally and

- through unambiguous advertising endeavors can increment deals and produce more brand mindfulness. Lead age straightforwardly affects deals once a lead converts to a client.

- Create a dream: Leading organization

development with a dream makes a make way for a business to grow. Since development is more probable through designated endeavors, making objectives that set up unambiguous drives can assist everybody in an association with pursuing achieving similar goals.

- Build your Brand: Build entrust with buyers by associating clients to your image. Making an arrangement to use social and different stages can assist with growing your business as well.

Chapter 3

Know Your Customer

Knowing your customers is key for any business to grow. Fruitful entrepreneurs comprehend what their clients need and the best approach to making their item or administration that anyone could hope to find. The profundity of information is likewise critical - it requires knowing more than their names, ages and livelihoods. As an entrepreneur, knowing your client's side interests, tastes and interests alongside what they watch, pay attention to and peruse can be a productive benefit.

Understanding your client's purchasing conduct is additionally vital. As an entrepreneur, you really want to grasp what kind of individual is probably going to need or need the item or administration you give. These are a portion of the key inquiries that fruitful entrepreneurs need to ask themselves consistently:

What is their justification for buying your item or administration?

How frequently would they say they will have to purchase that item or use the assistance? In the event that you can be proactive with your effort endeavors around the time you realize they will buy, odds are the client won't look somewhere else.

Who are they purchasing for? Your informing and advancement will be dependent upon assuming that they are buying for themselves or for another person.

Where are they probably going to buy? In the event that you are a physical business and hear from your clients that they would like to arrange on the web, then, at that point, it's a good idea to change your plan of action to incorporate a web based business or web based requesting part.

Organizations that understand what their clients need and what they expect can likewise chip away at tweaking the client experience to make steadfastness and rehash business. More modest and all the more fast to-answer business people and entrepreneurs as of now have the high ground for accomplishing this upper hand. Basically by expanding the length of your client's cooperation will give a more prominent chance to make a positive encounter and fabricate areas of strength for a. Pay attention to your client's input and give sound counsel, regardless of whether you in some cases need to guide your client to another source.

As an entrepreneur, it is critical to take each benefit to outfox your rival, and understanding and expanding upon your client information and relationship will put you on top of things

Realize your customers better on the grounds that no one but them can assist you with getting more lead and more business.

Understanding clients is the way to giving them great assistance which thus results serious areas of strength for into connections and new deals through sure verbal exchange suggestion. In any case, understanding the clients' mind is difficult and most frequently requires a smart examination to recognize their inclinations or buy designs with the goal that you can expect their necessities and surpass their assumptions.

Chapter 4

The role of TRUST in Business

It's difficult to evaluate precisely the way that significant trust is for a business. For entrepreneurs, an absence of trust is your greatest cost. It might require a long time for a director or a leader to foster the trust of their representatives, however just minutes to lose. Without trust, exchanges can't happen, impact is annihilated, pioneers can lose groups and sales reps can lose deals. The rundown goes on. Trust and connections, substantially more than cash, are the money of business.

Trust is the normal consequence of thousands of small

activities, words, considerations, and expectations. Trust doesn't occur at the same time; acquiring trust takes work. It could require long stretches of approaching a specific client to get through and completely gain their solace and trust. However notwithstanding the significance of confidence in the business world today, not many pioneers have given it the concentration and supporting it merits.

Business planner David Horsager talks universally on the main concern effect of trust. He has fostered a framework with which he shows pioneers how to construct the Eight Pillars of Trust:

Lucidity - People trust the reasonable and question the equivocal

Sympathy - People put confidence in the people who care past themselves

Character - People notice the individuals who make the wisest decision over what is simple

Capability - People trust

the individuals who stay new, applicable, and competent

Responsibility - People have confidence in the people who stand through difficulty

Association - People need to follow, purchase from, and associate with companions

Commitment - People promptly answer results

Consistency - People love to see the easily overlooked details done reliably

It is vital to comprehend that trust is key to the certifiable outcome of any sort. The trust you have with your group and associates, the trust you place in your sellers to make conveyances right and on-time, and the trust that you work to procure from your clients.

"The significance of trustworthiness and uprightness has forever been basic at Behler-Young. (As far as I can tell, this is all morally significant, yet it is likewise shrewd business." - Doug Young, Behler-Young President.

Also, it merits the work. Real trust yields

diminished pressure, strong kinships and an enduring heritage.
Trust is essential in business connections. It decides your outcome in business improvement. Do you battle to get your partners to work with you? Perhaps they have zero faith in you enough, and that is an issue in business improvement.

All things considered, as

business designers, we flourish with individual connections. In any case, if our accomplices, clients, or supervisors don't see us as reliable, they will not contribute their experience with us.

This implies you will not get associations, you won't close arrangements and your administrator won't be available to advancing you or in any event, keeping you in the group.

To put it plainly, finding success in business improvement begins with building trust. Fortunately you have some control over the manner in which individuals see you and be reliable in their eyes

Chapter 5

Follow up your

Customers

The demonstration of following up is essential for any business and without it, business will fail to exist.

From the beginning, I thought the expression "follow up" related exclusively to deals. As time continued and I developed in business, I observed that the demonstration of follow up is significant in every aspect of business. The most effective way I portray follow dependent upon myself is the method involved with finishing an action.

Follow up is the most common way of finishing a movement, so with regards to business, particularly when you really want to secure new clients, follow up implies transforming a possibility into a client. What's the significance here for the possibility? This truly intends that in the event that you don't follow up, you can't assist with tackling their concern.

Significance of follow up to customers and how you can make it happen.

At the point when you start another business

or delivery another item, your essential spotlight is on getting the news out across the market and whenever that is finished, potential clients try harder to get related with the new pursuit. In any case, that isn't the finish of the story! Regardless of the number of individuals you that draw in any case, they won't ever change over them into your clients with out opportune subsequent meet-ups. As it's been said, specialists who don't circle back to clients are overlooking large chunk of change.

Business - Marketing - Customers: 3 Interconnected viewpoints
Business promoting doesn't exactly mean leading appropriate statistical surveying and introducing your item in

the most potential tempting manner. As a matter of fact, showcasing techniques incorporate the basics of setting up a possible lead to purchase your item without leaving any qualms inside their psyches.

Following up your Customers is the most significant piece of any of your advertising techniques, which most advertisers neglect. Accordingly, I'm here to explain to you for what reason is it important to circle back to clients or possible leads. Here is a diagram which will illuminate the state of the clients who encountered no sort of subsequent meet-ups.

Subsequently, 65% of the clients soak up pessimism inside themselves about the organization. No clients will remain with you in the event that you let them be during tough spots, so now is the ideal time to follow up!

Significance of follow-up to customers: Assumption satisfaction At the point when you circle back to clients, you can know their inclinations and what they are anticipating from you. At the point when you can comprehend what your clients need you are likewise ready to furnish them with a quality item. Which furnishes them with more motivation to get your item.

Client's stick around Circling back to clients gives a feeling that you care about your clients and are accessible for them. To that end clients adhere to your business for a more drawn out timeframe as you are dependably accessible.

Causes clients to feel exceptional
All things considered, who despises exceptional treatment? Being a client I appreciate certainly standing out and dealt with like an exceptional person. At the point when my criticism is

asked it causes me to feel esteemed and I am expecting comparable is the situation with you. So subsequent meet-ups cause clients to feel exceptional and accordingly this expands the dependability interaction for the clients.

Makes marketing a stride ahead
Clients recollect you

until the end of their lives, for conveying extraordinary client assistance. 96% of the clients likewise concur that client support is a boundary to decide their decision of brand and furthermore their reliability towards it. As "follow-up" is the equivalent for client care, your clients with without a doubt discuss it with others. Consequently there's a high chance that your image could spread among others without even you being familiar with it (and there is nothing similar to certifiable informal). Hence, simple promoting.

www.ingramcontent.com/pod-product-compliance
Lightning Source LLC
Chambersburg PA
CBHW070248220526
45465CB00004B/1560